BARBARA POLLA

IVORY HONEY

NEW RIVER
PRESS

New River Press is an indie poetry press based in Fitzrovia, London. It publishes new work by new and established poets, and the open-submission *New River Press Yearbook* annually.

Copyright © NEW RIVER PRESS
First published in 2018
by New River Press London

thenewriverpress.com

set in Mrs Eaves
design and typesetting
by New River Press
drawings by Julien Serve
julienserve.com

ISBN: 978-1-9996310-0-0

To
you

INTRODUCTION— Frank Smith

The light that says
I've always been there
and you've always been there
and I've always loved you.
The light is that of her gaze,
it grows.
Yet no light absolutely
no light passes through the bodies,
their sexes,
their mouths,
their voices,
their cries.
What does it matter?
She is the first
to admit defeat
and she is the first
to start over,
and she is the first
to start over again.
She wants to flow
without veins,
an open way
of proceeding,
of saving the contours,
concluded from the scream itself.
The next thing will always be
to start over again,
from things to words
and from words to things,
she will not watch him
go,
anything go.
The thing grasps the word,
it is every time every night

in the world,
her syntax does that to her.

It is in the body-word then
that something happens,
a great cry in motion.
The mouth conquers everything
an envelopment of flesh,
there is a cry in the meat.
The mouth is everywhere, a sky, wind,
a stone in the head, burning skin,
love separated,
a dream blown away.

Her syntax does that to her
and it's a subject-object body.
She cries out at the invisible,
she cries out at those who cannot hear,
she cries out
at loss,
at reuniting.

With tactile hands around
his waist.

Frank Smith, 2017

IVORY HONEY

ME AND YOU

Take me
Raise me
Rain me
Drive me
Kiss me
Feed me
Teach me
Tell me
Keep me
Draw me
Sky me
Drawn me
Be me
Bath me
We me
Call me
Dream me
Dear me
Laugh me
Let me
Lit me
Like me
Lick me
Look me
Loose me
Moon me
Star me
Stare me
Breed me
Read me
Beat me
Bite me
See me
Sea me

Deep me
Tree me
Try me
Fuck me
Cry me
Night me
Hit me
Shit me
Kill me
Eat me
Love you

OH MY HANDS
to Julien Serve

I don't know what to do with my hands
Hold my baby hold my body
Touch your face or touch your cock
I don't know what to do with my hands

Plunge my thumbs into your eyes
And caress your brain from inside
Cook witchy potions with the right one
Write bad stories with the left one

I don't know what to do with my hands
Hide them in my bottomless pockets
Hide them in your pocketless bottom
Or walk on them, hand by hand

Cut them off and write with my eyes
Cut them off and worship my wrists
Then finally everybody could grasp
How handicapped I am

ROUEN

Four kids killed a fifth one
From behind. Two shots in his head
Then they burned the body
A sunny afternoon

They were all teens
Teens tender and void
Gorgeous kids the five of them
Who's going to die next

Four kids erased a fifth one
For no reason than anger
Or maybe not even
Anger fills the void

They were brothers and teens
The fifth one only teen
Fifteen to be precise
Forensically fifteen

Five kids in the country
Four men in a jail
In a short news item
It happened yesterday

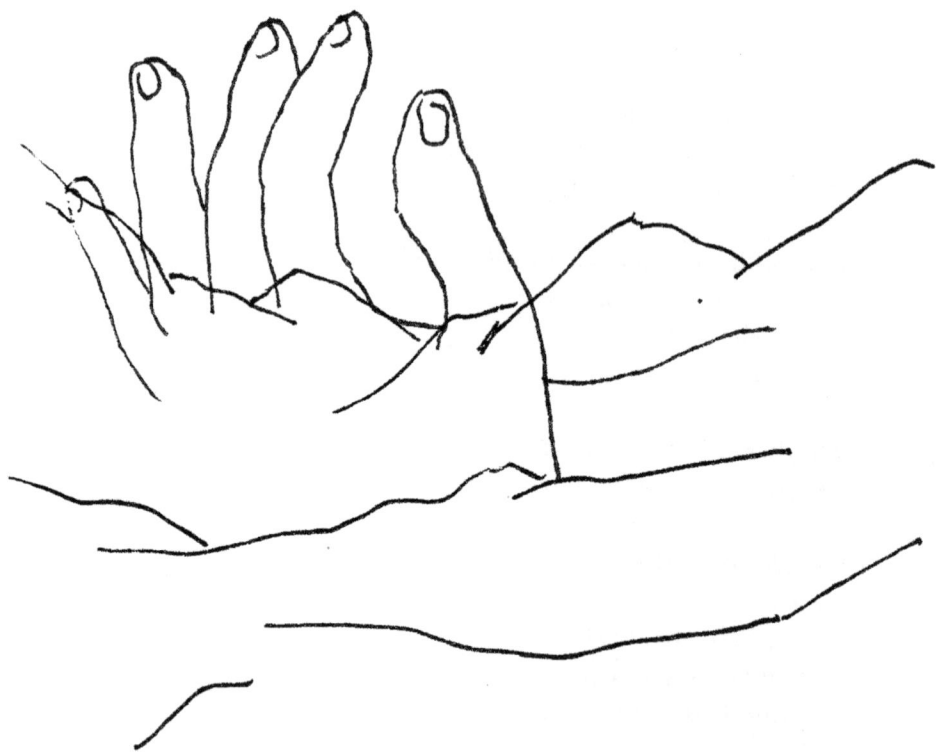

IN THE RAIN

I was lying on him
Him naked so was I
And his sperm in a cloud
Was dropping upon us
Like the tears in the rain

I was lying on him
He was like a boat
Floating boat in the fog
His mouth in my neck
Whispers in the rain

I was lying on him
Swimming on his body
Exploring geography
And he was like the sun
Shining in the rain

I was lying on him
I was loving his skin
Listening to his body
Listening to his mind
Singing in the rain

I was lying on him
Him naked so was I
And his sperm in a cloud
Was dropping upon us
Like the tears in the rain

CRYSTAL CLEAR

I draw his blood
From his veins
As a nurse
I hold his arm
And the needle
As a dealer

I drunk his blood, dripping over my chin
Onto my breast and nipples
Breast fed with sweet crimson blood
Drifting on my belly to my gluteal furrow
Between my thighs down my legs
And among my toes
I'm walking on his blood
Crystal clear crimson blood

From saliva to sperm from tears to piddle
And my favorite, cerebrospinal fluid I want
I can't eat his grey matter yet
But can collect the sperm of his brain
Lumbar puncture goes deeper than blood work
Cerebrospinal fluid ejaculates through the mandrel
Quenching my thirst at last my addiction
Crystal clear creamy life

I draw his sperm
From his penis
As a nurse
I hold his body
And the needles
As a dealer

Crystal clear

SINGING WITH THE WHALES
to Ursula

There are new genes emerging
From the shallow of the oceans
I can hear their genetic code
Singing with the wales
But I don't understand the words
The DNA alphabet seems to be changing
May be Chinese, may be Arabic
I need to learn new languages
Songs of yesteryear for to be
Singing with the wales
Millions of submarine woodpeckers
Hit the hulls of warships, flagships
Beached and aground tankers
Giving rhythm to the constant roaring of melting
And singing with the whales
Mutated genes offer biodiversity
Subaquatic plants talk AGTC in Japanese
Frightened seafarers scream ship ahoys
While inter-atlantic butterflies
Are singing with the whales
Autotrophic protists ingest new genes
New tastes they never knew before
Cooperate converse and drift in depth
And mute, mutate with the whales
While northern lights go south
Genes can talk walrus morse code
Transpose octaves and play the drums
Mitochondrial DNA inverts the games
Female inheritance reshuffles cross-currents
And genetic chaos creates new songs

LEONIE

I am a shark a female shark
They call me Leonie
I am a shark I want a baby
I am captive with no male
I had intercourse years ago
Maybe centuries
On deep coral reefs and sandy bottoms
I am a shark a female shark
They call me Leonie
I thought a lot
How I could do it
The delight of babies
Start life again
On deep coral reefs and sandy bottoms
I'm reshuffling my DNA
Selecting beneficial mutations
I increase my library size
Concentrate on female genes
And mitochondrial DNA
I am a shark a female shark
They call me Leonie
I made love to myself
Because puppies need love
If plants can do it
I can do it too, parthenogenesis
On deep coral reefs and sandy bottoms
We are four of me now
All female sharks
In my female world
I'm ready to meet males again
On deep coral reefs and sandy bottoms
I am a shark a zebra shark
They call me Leonie
And no one understands

SHIVER AND SHAKE

She was called Albertine
At three got abandoned
At nine got abused
Fifteen heroin
Twenty one went to jail
Los Angeles angel
Down the hill right to hell
After hell and years later
Landry Strohl lyrica
Shiver and shake

She was called Albertine
And we sat Place des Vosges
And her legs shivering
In my hands let it go
Pregabalin darling
I love her to death
Black desire suicide
She is mad so am I
Red roses on her bed
Making love on prescription

Shiver and shake
For how long will we stand
This acute pain to soul
Screeching ghosts down the trees
Screaming ghosts on the lawn
Place des Vosges
Piano bar through the night
Piano love through the pain
Pregabalin darling
She was called Albertine

CALL ME RED
to Selen

I was born in Ventura
South of Santa Barbara
Los Padres were just there
Then moved to Culver City
To enjoy incongruity
From Jurassic Technology
Then flew to Germany
With overzealous spirit
In search of pigeon markets
As I knew — call me Red —
That my pigeon was somewhere
Between Bosphorus and Spree
In the face on unfathomable phenomena
She was living on Lyrica
Took the Berlin-Bagdad railway
To Konya Adana never ending in Bassorah
Lyrica makes her sleep Lyrica makes her laugh
Men over there don't treat her well
They keep her in a place
That was called Innocence
She has metal in her hands
Innocence without boarders
Flying back returning home
I was born in Ventura
Ojai's my pigeon's nest and she's my rain dove
She's a warrior with a compass — sending
Transpacific letters to California forests
From Ventura to Monterey fire alerts everywhere
Los Padres call me Red and my rain dove
Flew away — our journey's never ending.

DÉSORDONNANCE

Désordonnance de désobéissance
Depuis la plus petite enfance
Jouer nu dans la boue
Embrasser les passantes
Amplifier le désordre
Ne pas réussir
Chanter faux à tue tête
Chanter tue, faux, tête
Crier dans la nuit hululer Dormicum
Hurler à la lune être lune et l'autre
Viande crue d'animal inconnu
Ne pas réussir
Désordonnance de désespoir
Se blesser aux choses en riant
Des sabres émoussés des tessons dissonants
Traverser la cour de l'école
Pieds nus Haldol
Ne pas réussir
Manger toutes les langues
Langue d'Oc langue d'eau
Dos salé do de mer, mer de feu
Langue de bœuf ou de porc de Babel funambule
Terre brûlée Xanax
Ne pas réussir
Désordonnance d'insomnie
Somnambules inguérissables
Rêveurs de jour rêveurs de nuit
Joueurs de flûte lutte enchantée
Butobarbital — but t...
Ne jamais s'endormir

RED LIKE A SUMMER NIGHT

My heart is full of blood
My blood is full of gravel
Thick and hurtful
There's blood in my body
There's blood everywhere
Running leaking flowing sinking
Singing

My eyes have seen the sun
Red like a summer night
My eyes in darkness
Blinded by the light
Black blood

My veins are blue of blood
Wrong toxic color
The heroes' blood is red
I'm missing oxygen
Polluted black breath

My tongue is red and blue
Beaten on the left side
My mouth is full of gravel
Thick and hurtful
My furred tongue
Black tongue henceforth
On the left side

On the left side of my chest
My heart is full of blood
Heavy like a coal scuttle
My heart's turning black

My words are singing high
My words are full of blood
Red like a summer night
My words are never black

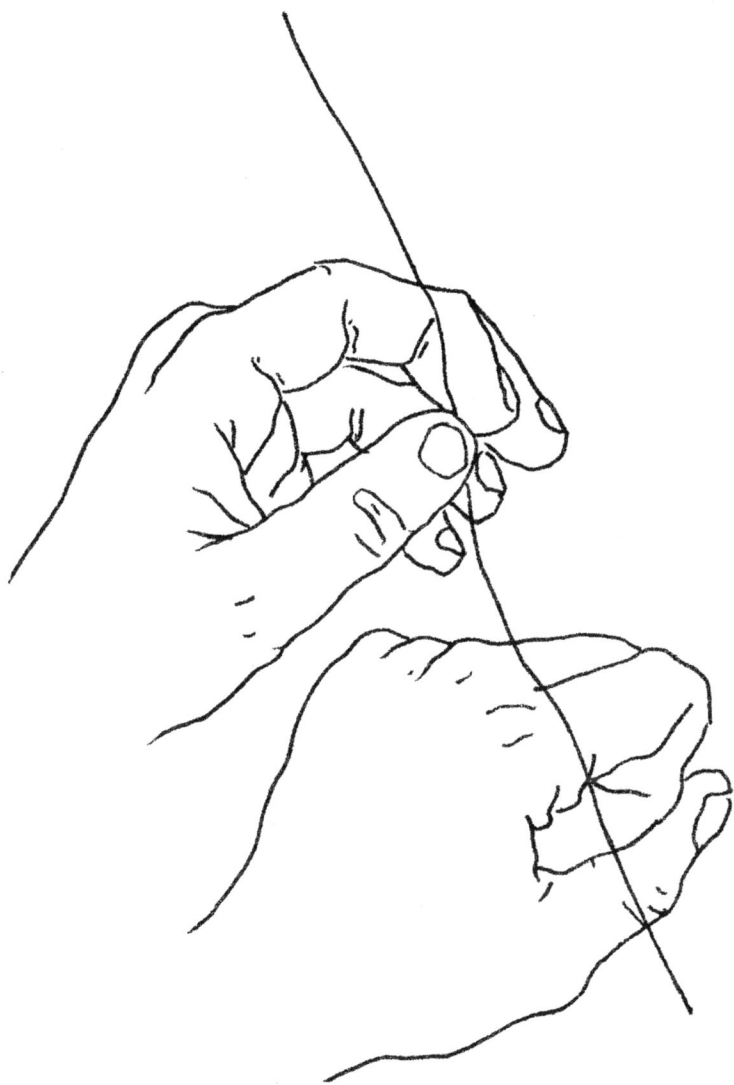

MY LOVE IS A DRAGON
to Ada and Edwin

My love is a dragon
He spits fire when he talks
Forest fires when he kisses
Sunset blaze looks at me

My love has three heads
Two wings like a blackbird
He's a dream creature
His teeth are firefighting

My love frightens the world
My dragon protects me
Between the wings of my love
The blue sky as his playground

My dragon is of fire
Born in nineteen sixty-six
Dignified and passionate
But the Christians killed him

They killed him many times
Saint George in particular
But his heads always re-grew
He had three, now sixteen

Sixteen heads were not enough
George killed him for true
His blood filled the Red Sea
I went bathing there

I could smell my dragon's blood
He's buried in my dreams

I could feel my dragon's ashes
Rebirth is for tomorrow

And the next day he was back
With thirty seven heads
Dozens of black wings
And fire everywhere

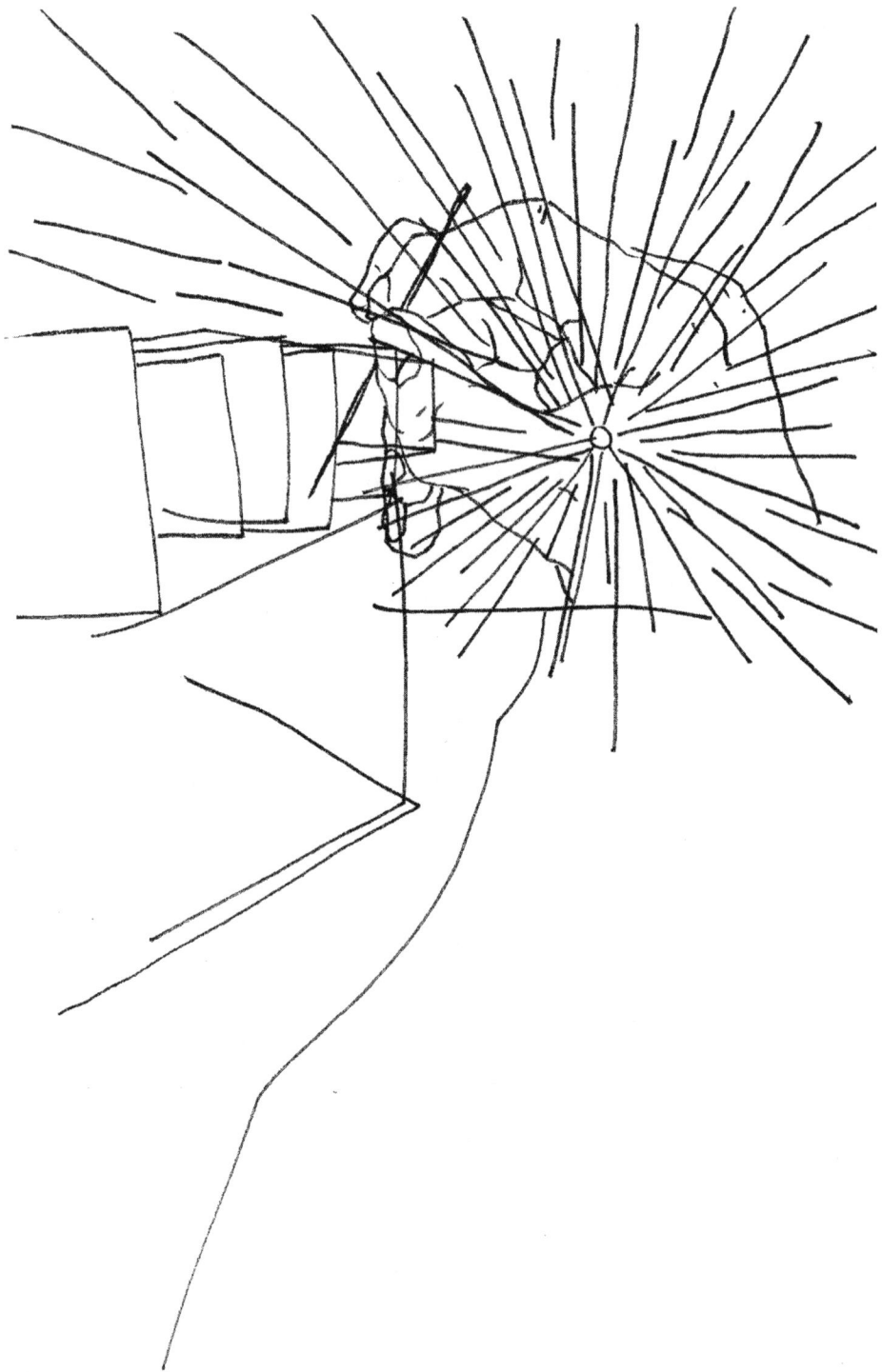

THERE IS FIRE EVERYWHERE

I love you, you fuck me
If not you, then life maybe

I love you for your lips
I love you for your cock
I love you for your fuck
I love you for your pains

I love you, you fuck me
If not you, then life maybe

I love you for your pains
For your endless shitty belly
For your words for your songs
For there's nowhere to go

I love you, you fuck me
If not you, then life maybe

For there's nowhere to go
Turning home in despair
Miss you here miss you there
There is fire everywhere

I love you, you fuck me
If not you, then life maybe

URBAN NIGHT
to Nicolas T

We met on the street
Night urban time
Don't want to go home
It's friezing cold
The void

Let's go for
One more drink
One more drug
One more life
One more wife
Another knife

He walked through the city
With painful knees
Thought of flowers
And drunk the fuel

No angel down the street
His youth has gone
His body's wet
The meadows in his head

Let's howl for
Another drink
Another drug
Another life
Another wife

Another night
Freezing knife

A LAUGHTER IN MY BED
to Pradeau

He was curious
And fast
Like an angel
Unconscious
His hands on my body
His palms so soft
A laughter in my bed
Then darkness

Now I know the shape of his cock
In the early hours of dawn
When men sleep while I'm awake
But don't know the color of his eyes

He was like an incest
An angel a homeless
A rising sun
An unknown alien
A laughter in my bed
A kid on a cloud
Too fast grown out
And vanished

Now I know the deep beating of his chest
In the darkest hours of night
When kids sleep and I'm awake
But don't yet know his name

HYDRANGEA

Last night I saw
White flowers in the dark
Immense and glowing like a moon
In the meadow last night

I picked them up
Broke the stalk
Bleeding stalk
Wound my knees
Bleeding knees
Down to earth
Bleeding moon

Bleeding moon hydrangea
And white petals in the night

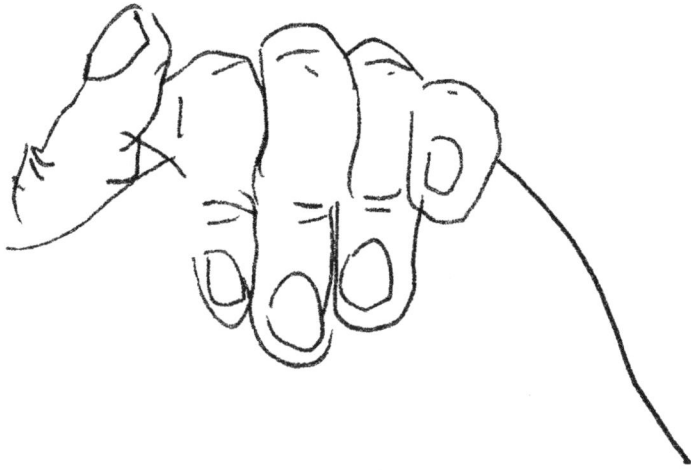

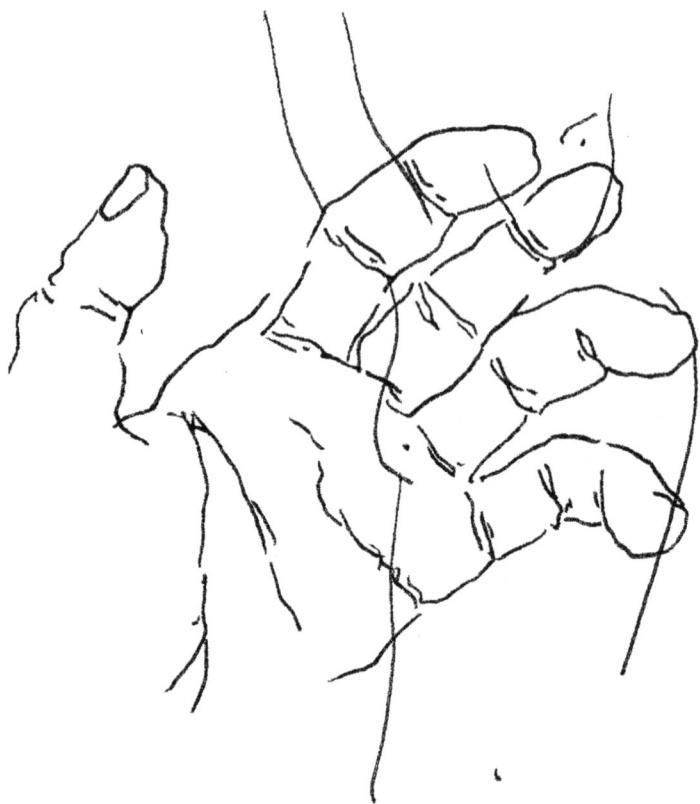

L'ÉLÉGANTE

L'élégante buvait seule
Et avec son amie
Son amie le tambour
Buvait en compagnie
Et tapait le tambour
De ses longs ongles jaunes
Ses scories sous ses ongles
Des cheveux et des poils
Le tambour le tambour
Son bonnet sur la tête
Velours à deux chaînes
Elle chantait au tambour
Ses restes entre ses dents
Dupuytren dans ses mains
Et l'eau dans son ventre
Qu'elle n'avait jamais bue
Son ventre comme un tambour
Et ses longs ongles jaunes
Qui dessinaient un monde
D'une grande élégance
Son ventre d'éléphant
La chaleur de son corps
Glacé comme une orange
Les vapeurs les odeurs
Le tambour qui frappait
Son amie le tambour
De velours déchaîné
Et rythmait le monde
Avec grande élégance

THREE MEN IN A BAR

Three men in a bar
They talk prostitutes
And laugh

CHARLOTTE & BLEY

Do you know this place?
Swamp and saltern — they call it Marais
Live Hugo condemned death penalty
But years after he died
Five hundred kids were deported
It says so on the walls of the school nearby

Late at night music and voices
All the voices on hearth
And the fans on the ceiling
Turning around like wind turbines
And the wind and music in my ears

Do you know this place?
I met him here at dusk
But couldn't really see him
And he said - What did he say?
Something about life
But the words got lost in the music and the wind
And I just remember a color

Yellow in the twilight
A pin oak is growing
In the middle of the room
With coffee beans and salad leaves
And on the walls it says
In case of emergency
Call Café Charlot

Do you know this place?
Late at night
Carla Bley sings Leçon Française
The girl who cried champagne
And I dance with her to forget about him
To forget those kids
To fly with the birds

And hand-pick marsh marigold

TOMORROW

Tomorrow I will tell you
Tomorrow I will sing
For the rain in your hair
For the blue of your eyes
The women in your life
Your transatlantic journeys

Tomorrow your curls
Will unfold in my hands
And the smell of your body
Will turn sweet on my lips
And your feet in my mouth
Walk thousands of miles

And the shine of your smile
Will melt the stones
There's a hole in your heart
Your blood down the drain
Tomorrow you will tell me
That you don't love me

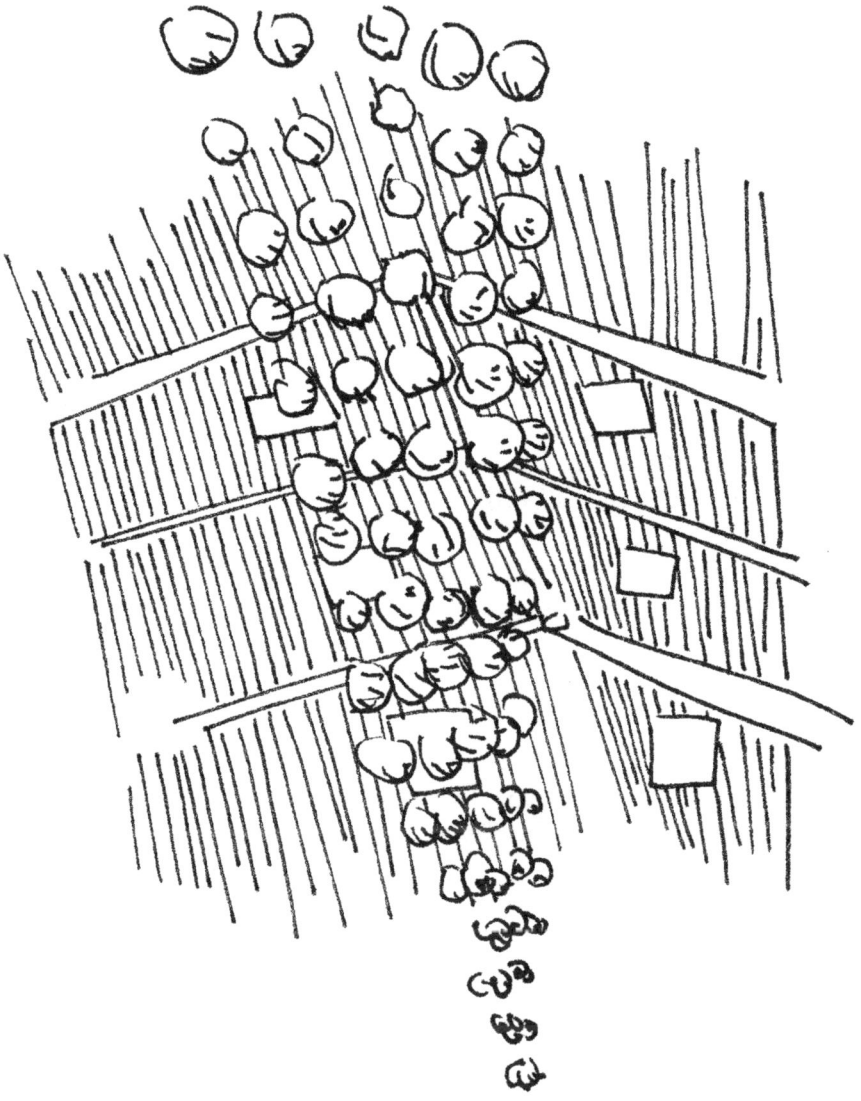

THE LIZARD IN HIS BRAIN

He's a stone with blue eyes
And sometimes he smiles
He's a man with a brain
And sometimes he sings
Songs with no words
Smelling green like the lizard
The lizard in his brain

He's a man with green eyes
And he's walking through the desert
Singing like a dog
And barking in his brain
And biting the snakes
The green snakes and the apples
And the lizard in his brain

He's a dog and he barks
He's a man and loves cars
Green cars and death machines
With a snake as a collar
Around his tiny neck
A sweetheart having sex
And the lizard in his brain

The snake caught the lizard
And the stone smashed the snake
And he swallowed the apple
His blue eyes full of tears
He's lost in the desert
And the dog and the car
It's fun to be dead

With a stone in his brain

UNCANNY

My love is in the wind
My kid is on the swing
And I'm under the wings
Of angels uncanny

Birds are flying north
The sky is burning high
Behind another sky
Your hand in your curls

My love is in the wind
My kid is on the swing
Angola Missouri
The doors will open soon

Mississippi under water
River is burning deep
I don't know where I am
But my kid is on the swing

Double edged sword
My paths in the high grass
Behind a cloudy sky
My love is in the wind

Your taste is in my mouth
Your name is on my lips
And I'm under the wings
Of angels uncanny

SAD MAN
to James

Sad man
Walked by the lake
Silver lake
Gloomy life
Somber thoughts

Sad man
Took off his clothes
Jumped in the lake
Swam to exhaustion
Near drowning

Sad man
Took off his life
Took off his thoughts
Kept his body
For free

Naked man
Ran by the water
Silver water
Frozen body
Alive

I'M ALIVE
to Larry Lucky Sultan

I am Lucky
I'm alive
Could be dead
On the floor

I'm a cowboy
I'm a man
I've lived long
And want more

I am Lucky
She is Kelly
Flowers blossom
In her hair

There is spring
On the beach
There is spring
In my mind

Could be dead
In the waves
But I'm Lucky
I'm alive

OUR WINTER OF 2010
to Alexander McQueen with thanks to Frank Perrin and Sam Samore

Alexander hung himself
To the red thread of their lips
As if they were processions
Funereal and flamboyant
We understood, Alexander
That you wouldn't go any further
You lose her and the thread
She gave out her last card.
Grandiloquent Gorgon
Overwhelming and macabre
Our winter of 2010

The clown hung himself
In flamboyant make-up
White corolla dark sight
Between yeast contaminated walls
In borderless hinterland
Living an obscure life
Obscure and flamboyant
The clown sang
Let me, let me
Freeze to death
Our winter of 2010

The Queen hung herself
But the rope let go
And the blood coagulates
The muddy territories
Of garishly painted faces
These womens' faces
In slimy disguise
And death is behind you
And death in front of us
Flamboyant victory
Of our winter of 2010

UNDER THE SKIN
to mounir fatmi

Under the skin the human soul
Under the skin the body the organs
Under the skin the colours faint
In red like blood and pink like flesh
Under the skin we all look black
Black as in Brodsky's poems
Inside us he says it is black I believe
Black like me
John Griffin who are you?
Your ID doesn't tell
Immigration I guess some centuries ago
Welcome to darkness memoir of blindness
Blinding light changed the colors
Black and white white like me
Inverted mirror shows me faint
Without you I would have died
Shadowless surgical light
Red like blood and pink like flesh
Graft a leg graft a soul
Under the skin the human soul

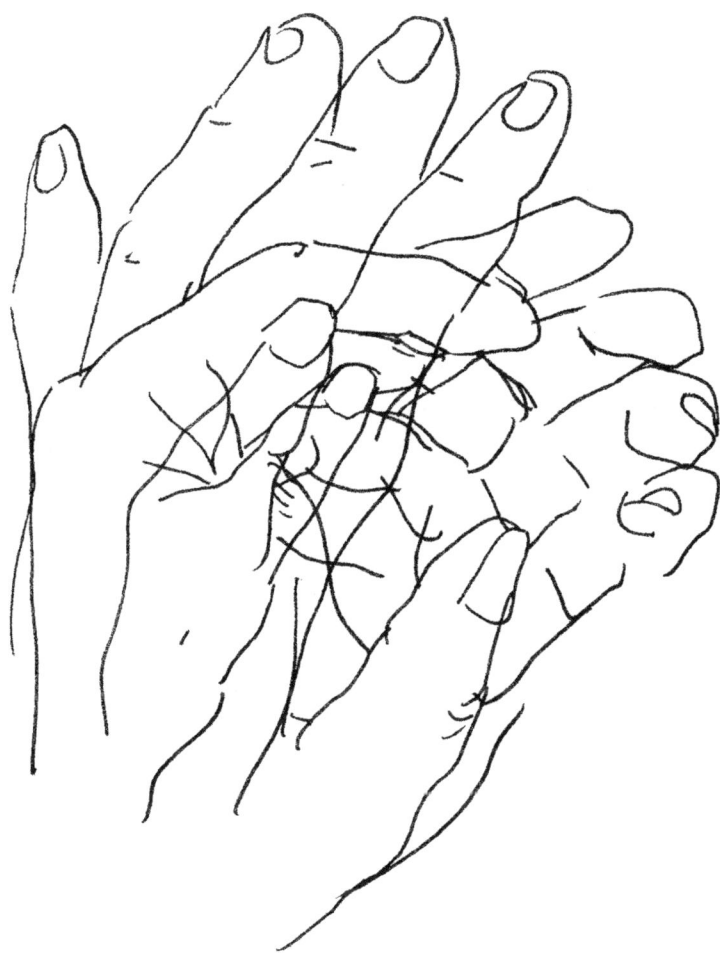

TENDER AND BRUTAL

Between my thighs
Love is running
He's coming in
Tender and brutal

On a beach in Rome
They killed Pasolini
Kids with no thoughts
Him tender and brutal

Freezing wind
My thighs warm and wet
The bike is running fast
Tender and brutal

On a stair in Odessa
The boots of Tsarist soldiers
Were killing and killing
Brutal and brutal

Between my thighs
Love is running
Life still living
Tender and tender

TING-A-LING-A-LING

On the boat in the sky
Peter Pan Tinkerbell
Floating high undergrowth
Under curls down to earth
Empty and naked
Kids dream fake dreams
Ting-a-ling-a-ling

Behind a cloudy sky
On the moon on the boat
Tinkerbell Peter Pan
Black truffle perfume
Kids dream day time
Don't sleep any more
Ting-a-ling-a-ling

The Bells of Hell
Peter Pan Tinkerbell
Fake fairies of yesterday
Teens dying tomorrow
The moon in clear sky
Whenever an angel
Ting-a-ling-a-ling

The sun and the moon
Reflecting who's there
Tinkerbell's dreams
Peter Pan panic
John Giorno is screaming
Mowing the meadow
Ting-a-ling-a-ling

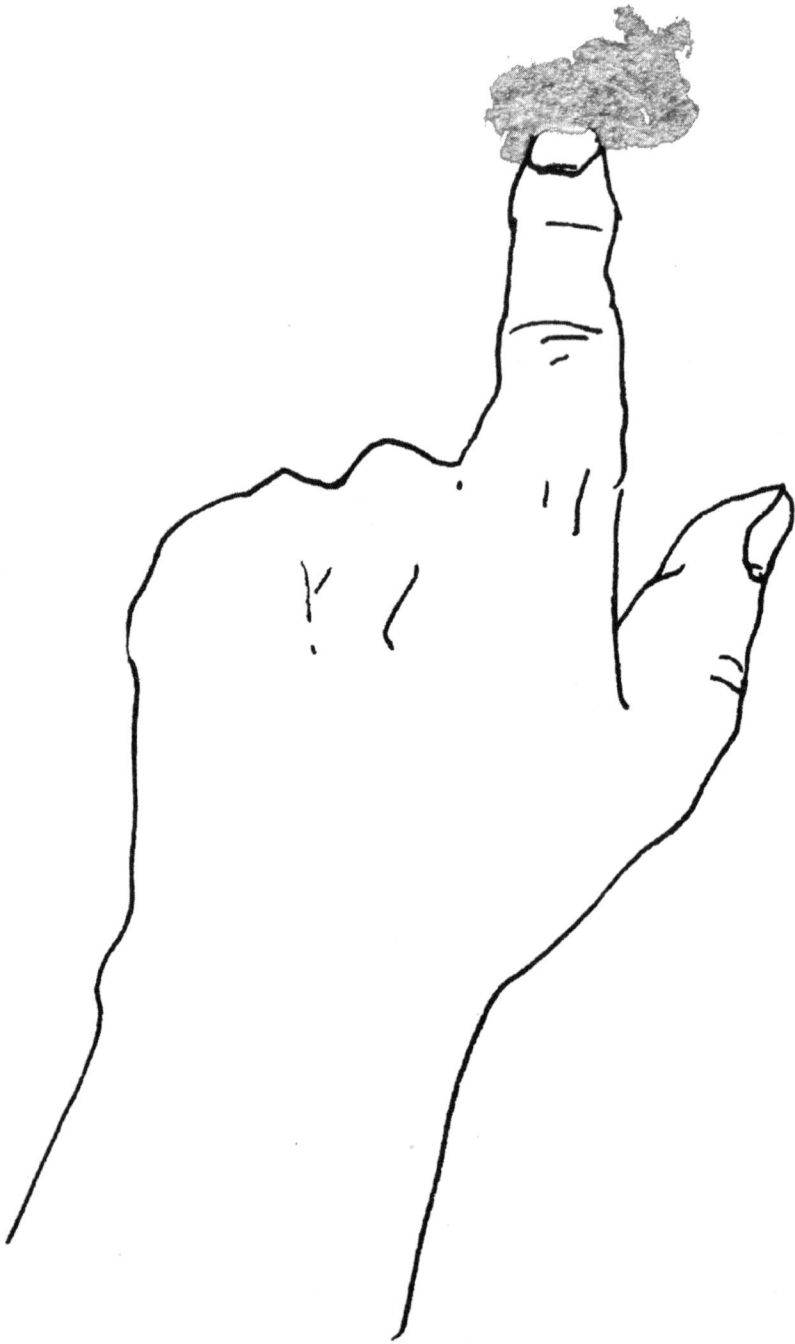

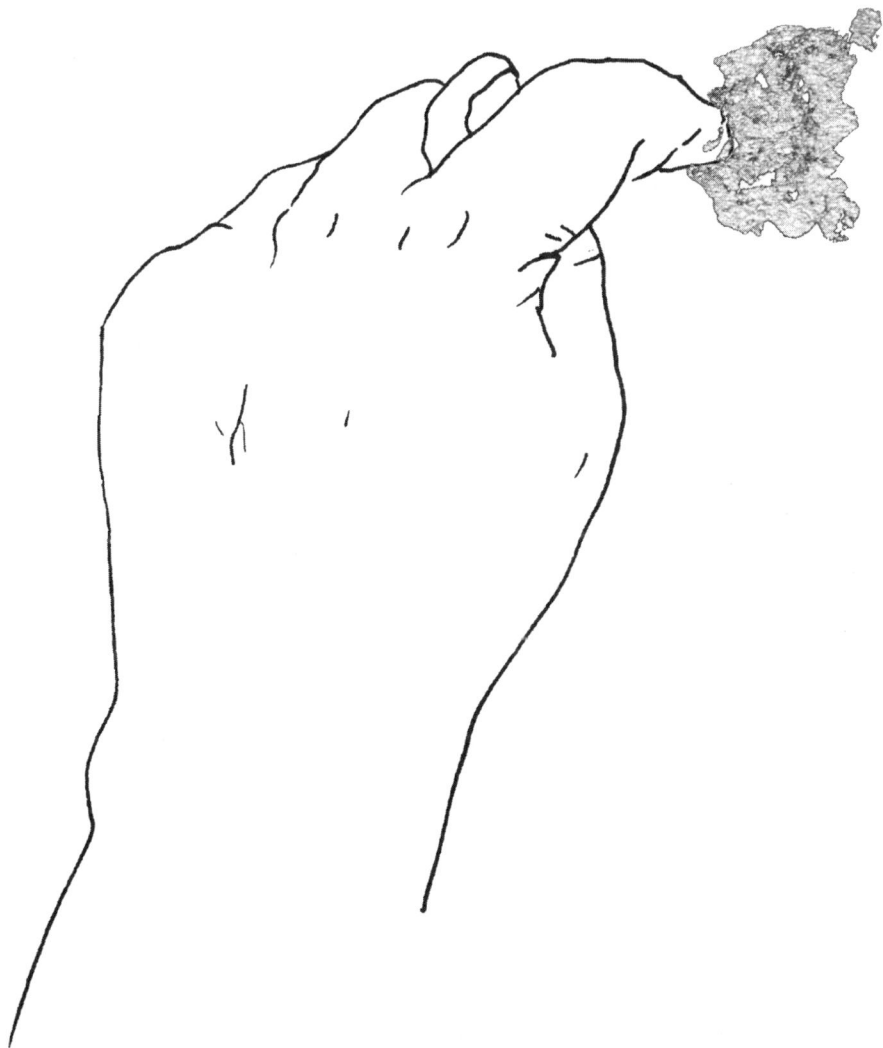

RÉPONSE À BRETON

Un homme aux cheveux d'airain
Et boucles de pain
A la pensée de cavalier
Un homme aux dents de tigre
A la bouche de volcan de fumée et de feu
Aux dents d'empreintes dans la chair des hyènes
A la langue odorante d'écorce montagnarde
Homme à la langue d'oubli d'appétit
A la langue de parole qui dit et qui se tait
A la langue de marée encore une fois salée
A la langue de saveurs
Homme aux cils comme des herbes folles
Dans les prés oubliés de la fin de l'été
Homme aux tempes d'ardoise ou l'esprit s'inscrit
Et de verre dépoli
Homme aux épaules de cheval de trait
Qui laboure nuitamment les terres du milieu
Déracine des rochers qui ressemblent à des corps
Homme aux poignets qui conduisent les chars
Aux mains de sculpteur de terre et d'argile
Aux doigts de plume au doigté d'arme blanche
Homme aux aisselles marines après la pêche
De nuits d'hiver où l'eau sent sous la glace
De graines de fougères de chemins ensablés
Aux bras de branches des arbres arrachés
Et de mélange de cimes et d'engrais
Un homme aux jambes de forêt
Aux mouvements du temps et d'ailleurs
Aux mollets de fougères près des sources
Un homme aux pieds signature
Aux pieds de talon d'Achille aux pieds des prés humides
Un homme au cou d'avoine odorante
A la gorge de torrent jurassique
De rendez-vous dans le lit même du torrent

Au torse de nuit
Un homme au torse de constellation lactée
Au torse de la force de l'or Paracelse
Un homme au ventre du creusement de soi
Au ventre de plaie béante
Un homme au dos d'hippocampe
Au dos d'étoile de mer dos de lumière
A la nuque de sel marin de marée descendante
Et de perte à jamais du contrôle de soi
Un homme aux flancs de vaisseaux
Aux flancs de Rackham le Rouge
De pirates au plus noir de pirates d'eau bleue
Un homme aux fesses de rocher
De marbre de Carrare
Aux fesses de collines en hiver
Aux fesses de neige
Au sexe de printemps
Homme aux yeux d'effroi
Aux yeux de corps aux yeux d'adieu
Aux yeux qui savent aux yeux qui jouent
Qui se ferment et revoient
Aux yeux d'eau qui se perd
Aux yeux de niveau d'eau de niveau d'air et de terre
Aux yeux de niveau d'eau sans jamais une larme

TEEN
to Sadegh Souri

I am thirteen
I am a teen
Time gives me body
And breast and blood
Desire for love
Desire for life
From inside me
Like a sun in my chest

I am thirteen
Have smuggled drugs
Have taken drugs
And killed my father
I should be hanged
At age eighteen
Waiting for that !

Five years to go
With death on row
They don't hang you
When you're thirteen
Five years to live
To eat to shit
To dream to screen
Five years to grow

You will all die
But you don't know
I am thirteen
Inside a jail
With walls and ropes
To close the time
How do you live

How should I live

This single life
I have received
With love for life
Inside of me

EXECUTION
to S M

He was sweating in tears
Dancing reciting
Stamping mad
Performing rage
Dripping tears
dripping sweat
dripping blood
dripping sex
He was counting the stars
Talked to the moon
Screaming to the sky
Black matter in his hands
Wide-eyed hobgoblin
staring big bang
the moon in the fog
and eight minutes later
Execution!

GATE OF TEARS
to Guendalina Salini & Italo Calvino

From the Libyan coasts
It took her just few hours
To join the army boats waiting at the border
Moving to another planet
A journey to Sicily
Turquoise crystal clear viridian
She crossed curtains of tears
Moving to another planet
Bab-el-Mandeb Catania
Where was she from again?
May be from Kordofan
Maybe from Kaduqli
During crossing she could see
Deep through the sea her brothers piling up
Giving life to new species
And translating DNA into further human hopes
She crossed curtains of tears
Dry tears from the desert
Bab-el-Mandeb Catania
Where was she from again?
The Italians are geniuses they welcome the tears
On this planet they drift into rivers
Then become lakes Gornalunga Gurnaza
They build invisible cities
Further north in the mountains
Esmeralda is for trading and Eudoxia for the sky
If on a winter's night a traveler

JOY IS EVERWHERE
to Abdul Rahman Katanani

Kilometers of barbed wire

entangle the earth

the earth revolves

the earth goes sour

joy is everywhere

humans live on earth

they live entangled

they live in camps

then bugger off

joy is everywhere

kids' play grounds

leaves of olive trees

mushrooms in the forests

all became barbed wire

joy is everywhere

gold glows on the walls

of palaces and camps

solar spectrum makes them shine

alike

solar spectrum makes them live

joy is everywhere

the shadows and the ghosts

of millions of humans

dissolve in the mirrors

like snow in the dust

joy is everywhere

comes the tornado and takes it all with it

the dust and the shadows

the trees and the kids

dashes to the sky

stays stuck on the ceiling

joy is everywhere

DID WE?

It was one night
We slept together, did we?
I sneaked in his bed
He was warm and good smelling
Soft skin big hands
He sort of woke up
Then his hands were everywhere
He turned me around
Onto my right flank
He's left handed that's why maybe

It was like taking a boat
And sailing afar
On some remote beach
Lying on the sand
Wrapped in silk and the foam of the daze
The foam of that night
His sex inside me
Somewhere below I don't remember where
It was fast it was slow
It went soft it went swing

Adrift
Downhill a dune
He fell asleep turned to the left side
He's left handed that's why maybe

I followed through the sheets
To end up in the morning
On another land
Another gulf another sand
Another dune another drift
Another dream
Come on get up
Before you fall
It was that night
We slept together, did we?

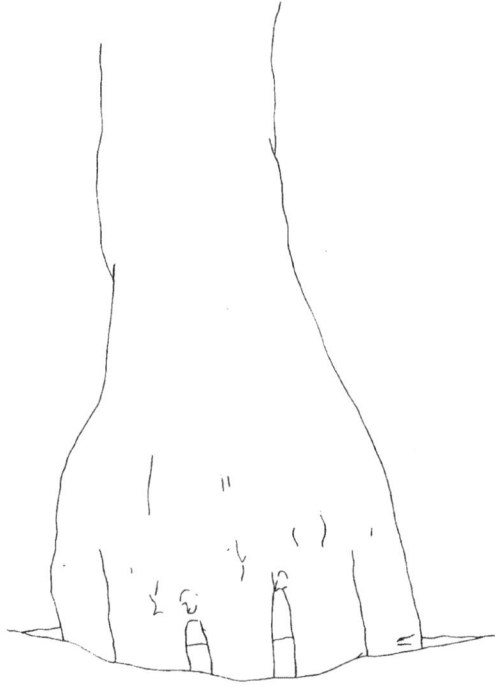

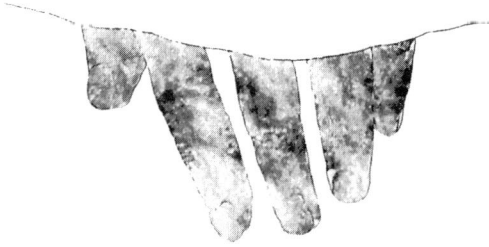

IVORY HONEY

I adore when his power
Melts inside me
I'm a female I'm a man
Atomic fusion operates
I'm a male I'm a woman

I adore when his softness
Hardens inside me
When he whispers to my ear
His dirty delights
Molecular construction

I adore when he asks me
To lick my shit on his cock
Sweet and salty
Organic constellation
Before the ivory honey

The snow is snowing on my garden
The snow is melting outside inside
They said we won't be able
Bellamacina wrote
To live on a pink cloud

So they said but we do live here
On that very pink cloud above my garden
Atomic fusion operates
Everything's melting in ivory honey
The snow and my body and the world and the clouds

I adore when his power
Melts inside me
I'm a female I'm a man
Molecular networks open the sky
And souls get lost in ivory honey

HANNIBAL
to Fabrice M

Un homme qui court un homme qui danse
Et qui ment

Un enfant

dans la salle de projection de son cerveau endormi
les rêves font défiler ses souvenirs d'antan
il porte son père sur ses épaules
et son fils dans ses bras

son père, marin échoué
lui dans le ventre de la baleine
il a quinze ans et essaie d'être un homme

il descend en ville les yeux de travers
il porte la montagne sur ses épaules
la faim est immense
le col de chemise plein de neige

le désespoir est au corps
comme un cancer
qu'on cherche à cacher à ses voisins
il porte son fils dans ses bras
et une contine dans son coeur

il s'en va déjà ?
non il s'accroche
aux flancs de la monatgne
à l'écume de l'enfance
aux têtards dans l'étang
la tête penchée
vers le diable au fond de la vallée

il joue avec lui et échange

les bouts de ficelles dans les poches de sa veste
contre quelques souvenirs de plus
le froid de la nuit contre la chaleur de son ventre
ses boucles de quinze ans contre une langue
les glaïeuls rouges contre une poignée de cailloux

Un homme dévale
il danse dans la ville
il est devenu fou un soir dans la montagne
dans la salle de projection de ses souvenirs d'enfant

Hannibal était passé par là

LOVE STORY

She is a crane
She loves her man
Her man is a crane man
He is her man

She is a dancer
A dancer in the night
Dancing proud and alone
Waiting for her man

He mounts her with joy
Every day of the week
Saturday night fever
She dances alone

He's inside her he's above her
She oversees the world
He loves her she loves him
She flies in the sky

Love is forever we all know that
Love until death the end of the feast
She loves the weights to work to turn
And crane men love the metal flesh

Machines and toys
And things and stuff
Be inside be outside
Protected and served

Crane men love dreams
And here she is
A dream machine
Flying in the sky

Beautiful and dreamy
She never complains
When he is with another
She dances in the night

EIGHT YEARS OLD

La nuit la pluie
Un homme des yeux
Dessine moi un éléphant
Le 395ème éléphant blanc
La poésie est toujours pour l'absent

L'étang s'est perdu
L'enfant fou et roi
Quand l'averse arrive son chant la précède
À la recherche de l'étang
La poésie est toujours pour l'absent

L'histoire est ailleurs
Elle nous aura manqué
Je pose ma tête comment poser sa tête
Le miel de l'aube fête
Et l'herbe entre les pavés

Merci pour rien
Je me souviens... le 395ème éléphant blanc
J'avais huit ans et à huit ans on n'oublie jamais rien
On n'oublie pas le lendemain
Les chansons sont toujours pour demain

And I'm still eight years old

Living like a wolf
Lonely in the night
Honey night

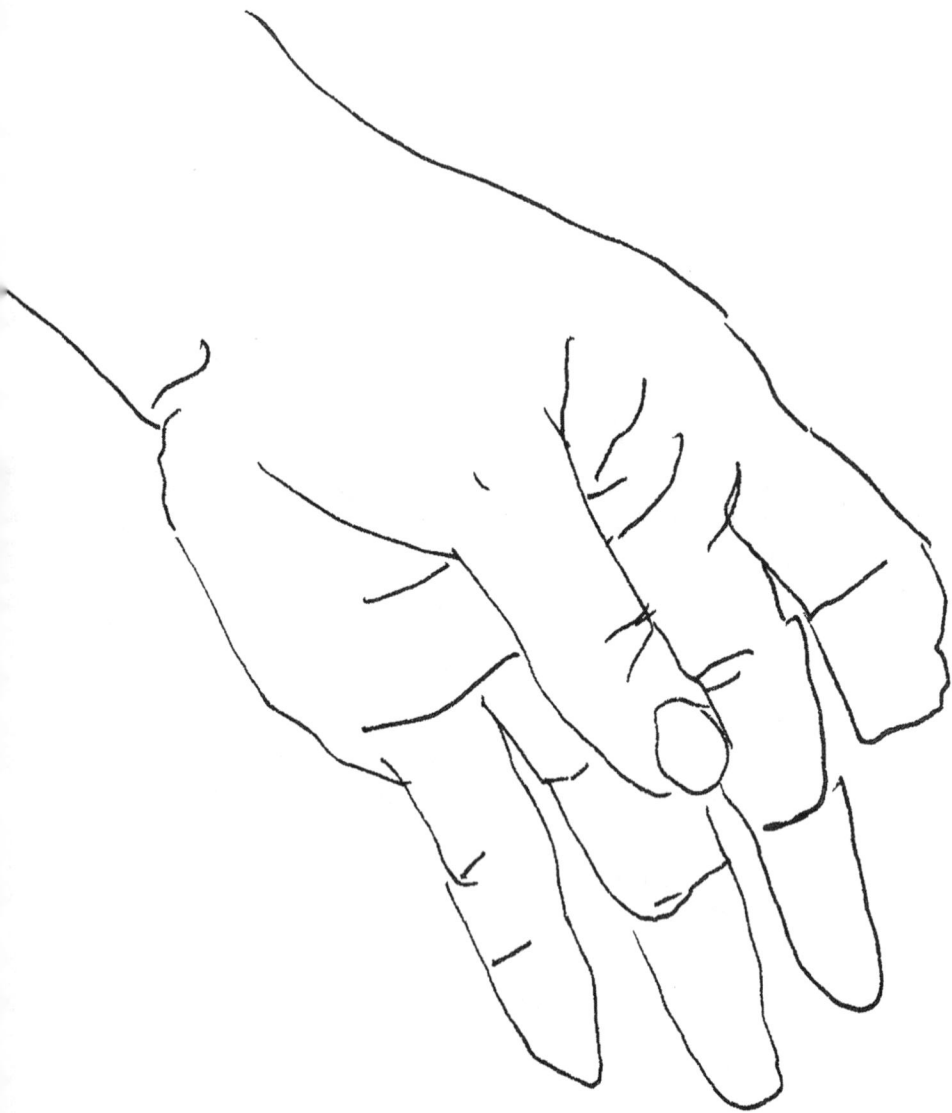

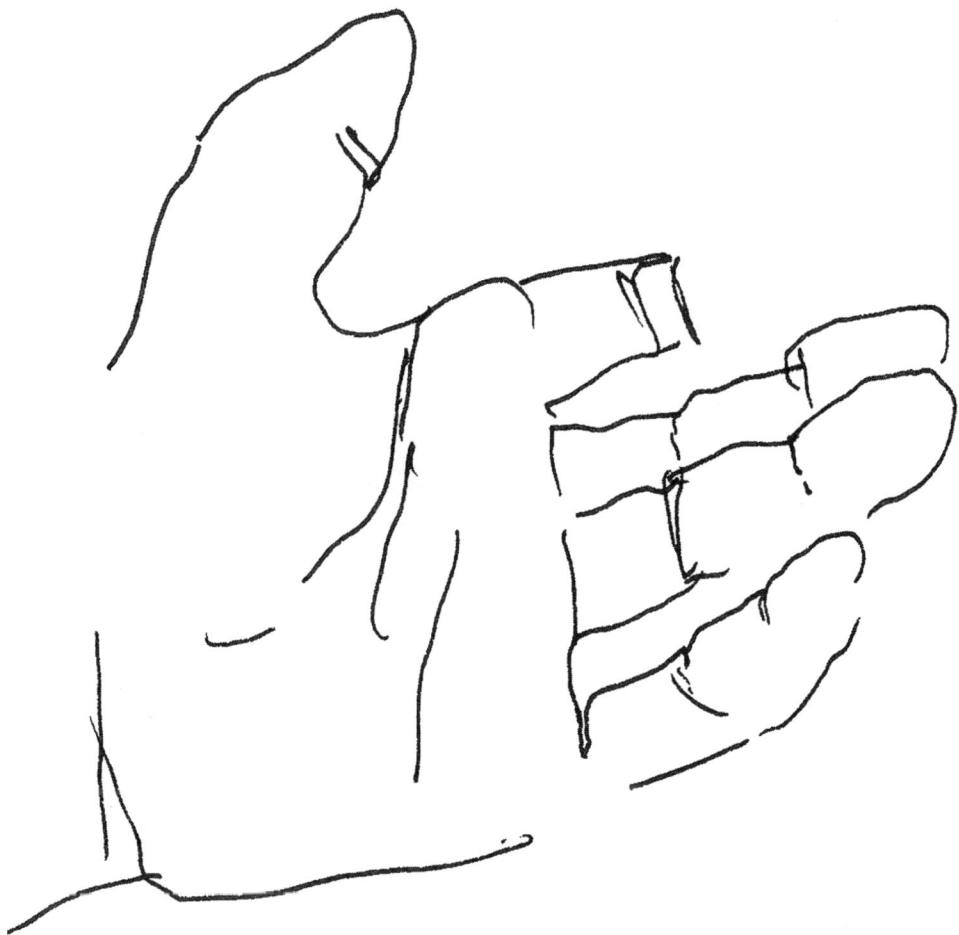

© Julie Borde

BARBARA POLLA began her career as a medical doctor and scientist working at Harvard and University Paris V René Descartes. She is the author of hundreds of academic papers published in *The Journal of Clinical Investigation* and *The American Journal of Physiology* and *The Proceedings of the National Academy of Science USA*. She was a Liberal MP in her native Switzerland, fighting for the abolition of prisons and abortion rights. Today she is a curator and owner of the innovative gallery Analix Forever in Geneva. She has written extensively on science, art, and gender in both French and English as well as several novels and various poetic prose. IVORY HONEY is her first collection of poems.

© Régis Figarol

JULIEN SERVE was born in 1976 in Paris, where he lives and works. He graduated from the Beaux-Arts Paris-Cergy. Serve explores every artistic medium but particularly drawing. He shows at the gallery Analix Forever in Geneva. The book of his collaboration with the poet Frank Smith, Pour Parler is published in spring 2018 by Creaphis Edition. "The hand draws the hand draws... The hand is almost a fetishist subject for me." Often Serve repeats the same motifs in a compulsive and monomaniac way modifying an element from a drawing to another, by changing a component, a composition, an association. Of his series on the hand he says, "The hand is the unlimited possibilities to hold divers tools. The hand is the condition of civilization on one side. It's also the first part of the body that touch the other. The hand is the node in which intersect society and intimacy. It thinks, builds, and also connects, feels, breathes."

More Poetry from New River Press:

Perishing Tame, Greta Bellamacina

To Die With Horses Wouldn't be so Bad, Zimon Drake

Branch and Vein, Rosalind Jana

Firing Slits: Jerusalem Colportage, Niall McDevitt

Coltash, Robert Montgomery

The Last Dodo and Dreams of Flying, Heathcote Williams

Points for Time in the Sky, Greta Bellamacina & Robert Montgomery

Smear: Poems for Girls, edited by Greta Bellamacina

Year of the Propaganda-Corrupted Plebiscites: New River Press Yearbook 2017 edited by Heathcote Ruthven

Selected Poems 2015-2017, Greta Bellamacina

available from **www.thenewriverpress.com**
and very selected bookshops

photo Fabio Paleari

NEW RIVER PRESS
PAPER TRINKETS FOR THE BROKEN—HEARTED

**HEATHCOTE WILLIAMS • GRETA BELLAMACINA
ROBERT MONTGOMERY • ZIMON DRAKE
ROSALIND JANA • NIALL McDEVITT • CHRIS McCABE
ROBERT LUNDQUIST • BARBARA POLLA**

www.thenewriverpress.com

NEW RIVER
PRESS

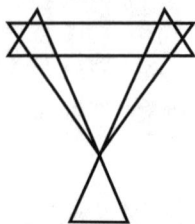

FITZROVIA
LONDON